# Grandpa's Memories of the Black Rock FOREST

## J. William Zoldak

Grandpa's Memories of the Black Rock Forest

Paperback ISBN: 9798218402082

Published by Stonehedges
OXFORD, MASSACHUSETTS

# Dedication

To Grayce Clark, friend and teacher.

# Dear Grandchildren,

I wrote this story about my memories of the Black Rock Forest located in my hometown of Cornwall, NY, to give you and other readers a picture of the forest during the bygone era of the 1950's and 60's. My hope is that you will be able to understand and experience through these adventures, stories, and photographs the magnificence of this special place. The photographs that are not identified were taken by either Will (my son) or me during a two-day hike through the forest in April of 2022.

VIEW OF BLACK ROCK FOREST FROM THE FIRE TOWER

OLD JAKE & AURELIA WITH 4 SONS (JACK, JOE, HARRY & ROBERT)

# Grandpa's Memories of the Black Rock Forest

*Introduction*

During the 19th and 20th centuries, the mountains on the west side of the Hudson River near Cornwall, New York (Storm King and Cro' Nest) were inhabited by old mountain families like Odell, Rose, Hagar, Chatfield, Hall, and Sutherland to name a few. These families owned small farms where they worked the land and raised their children. When they died, they were buried in small family cemeteries, sometimes in unmarked graves. For the most part, they were self-sufficient, producing all they needed to survive. To earn extra money, they would cut wood that they sold to brick yards, iron mines, and steamboat companies. Steamboats were common on the river in those days. It was because of this wood clearing practice, that by the beginning of the 20th century, there were virtually no old growth trees left along the Hudson River. Then as the railroad replaced the steamboats, the need for wood also diminished and the forests were reestablished with the new growth that exists today. The Black Rock Forest was formed out of these old family farms.

The connection between my family and the Black Rock Forest spanned several generations, beginning with my grandparents Jacob (Old Jake) and Aurelia (Burger) Zoldak. Aurelia moved to Cornwall just after the turn of the twentieth century as a child of twelve. In 1915, she met and married Jacob. Jacob had immigrated a few years earlier from Hungary and was working at West Point as a tailor. Soon afterward they opened a tailor shop on Main Street in Cornwall, that became a successful business for the next 40 years.  From their early days in Cornwall, they were fascinated with the mountains known later as the Black Rock Forest. Jake particularly liked the mountains because they reminded him of his home in the mountains of Hungary. As their family of four boys grew, they spent many wonderful days picnicking, fishing, hunting, and hiking in and around the forest.

Meanwhile, the Stillman family was purchasing the small farms and woodlands in the mountains as they became available. In 1928, Dr. Stillman formally established the Black Rock Forest and started an experimental forestry program. Jacob was Dr. Stillman's tailor at the time, so they were well acquainted. Then, sometime, perhaps during the 1930s, a severe forest fire was discovered in the forest. The forest manager at the time, Arthur Babcock, was ill with the flu and unable to respond to the crisis. He asked Jacob, whom he knew was familiar with the forest, to lead a group of volunteers to fight the fire. Jacob, of course, responded and eventually the fire was extinguished. From that time forward, Jacob was given a key to the gates to the forest and free access from a grateful Dr. Stillman.

For many years thereafter, old Jake and his family enjoyed the use of the forest with its many hiking trails, ponds, and scenic sights. I can remember as a small child going on blueberry picking trips from time to time. I'm pretty sure I ate more blueberries than I picked. As time passed and Old Jake died, that privilege was no longer available, but I always felt a connection to the forest. The Black Rock Fish and Game Club of which old Jake was a founding member, still has privileges in the forest. My understanding is that the first organizational meetings of the club were held in old Jake's tailor shop. Old Jake was a lifelong member of the club. Dr. Stillman died in 1946 and the forest was given to his alma mater Harvard University to continue the experimental forestry program he had started. My years in the forest were during these Harvard-owned years.

Although my family had this long relationship with the forest, my familiarity with it did not come through that source. My grandfather died when I was 15 years old, and he was sick with cancer for a long time prior to then. He was never able to share his knowledge with me. My father had spent time there as a boy but never really took me there as a child either. Fortunately, when I was about 8 years old, I started helping a lady by the name of Grayce Clark, a longtime resident of Cornwall, with her horses. As I got older, she would take me with her on trail rides in the forest. Because we lived on Angola Road, we would most often enter the forest from Secor's Hill (Mine Hill Road), although occasionally we would enter through the gates along Route 9W. From these trail rides, I learned the layout of the forest well. Later, during my teenage years after my family moved from Angola Road into town, I continued to spend time in the forest. I would either go on horseback using horses from Pop Cowton's stable (closer to Route 9W) or, more often, hike in with friends. I would have to say, however, that most of my knowledge came from Grayce, who was a wonderful friend and teacher. The following are memories/adventures of time spent in Black Rock during the 1950s and 60s.

# SECTION ONE
## Early Horseback Riding Days in Black Rock Forest

When I was 8 years old, my family moved to Angola Road. That is when I met Grayce Clark, a lady that became an important part of my life for the next 7 years. She owned a small stable nearby, where I worked. At first, she gave me small jobs like cleaning the stalls and brushing the horses. As I got older, I was given more responsibility until I was involved in the whole operation. At age 15 my family moved again. This time we moved into the town. I returned to the stable periodically at first, but my interests changed, and the distance discouraged my further involvement at the stable.

I have fond memories of those years living on Angola Road and working at the stable. Grayce was a good friend who not only taught me how to work with horses but many other life lessons as well. She also introduced me to the Black Rock Forest. The stories in this first section come out of that 7-year period. I reconnected with Grayce later in my adult years until she died at the age of 90.

GRAYCE CLARK – PHOTO THANKS
TO BETSY CLARK

BLUE BOY

# First Trail Ride in Black Rock Forest

My first exposure to the forest came in the early 1950's when I was perhaps 10 or 11 years old. By that time, I had been helping Grayce with the horses at her stable for a few years. I had learned to ride by then but only around the property surrounding the stable and under the supervision of Grayce as she instructed me. On many Saturdays during the warm weather, Grayce would saddle up one of the horses and go to the mountains for the day. Sometimes she would go with a friend but more often she would ride alone. I had hoped that one day she would ask me to go along, but up until then she had not. Then one day she surprised me with an invitation. I, of course, was delighted.

The following Saturday morning after the chores were done, we saddled up the horses and started on our way. Grayce was on Nugget, a newly acquired palomino, and I was riding Blue Boy, a 16-year-old blue roan that Grayce had owned for a long time. Blue Boy was a very accomplished trail horse who knew the forest every bit as much as Grayce did. To get to the forest, we rode along Angola Road and then up Secor's Hill (Mine Hill Road) to a trail that cut in at the top. Getting to the trail required crossing a small hay field owned by a lady who lived in the house adjacent to the field. She would forbid people from crossing the field because she said that they did destructive things to her property. Fortunately, she was more lenient with horseback riders. Otherwise, entrance would have been impossible. There was another trail that hikers took that was a steep climb over the mountain, but no horse could handle that rough terrain. Both trails converged about halfway in. Riding the horse trail was no easy task either. On this first ride in, we came to a steep, rocky, dangerous looking part of the trail that I was sure the horse couldn't handle. I stopped at the bottom of the slope and asked Grayce how we were going to proceed. Grayce simply told me to relax the reins and let the horse pick his way up the incline. She was right. He slowly picked his way along until we reached the top. Once the steep part of the trail was behind us, the path smoothed out until we reached Hall Road.

This entrance to the forest was seldom used and had many interesting sites along the way. There was mountain laurel everywhere as well as numerous small oak trees that were weathered by the wind. I later learned that these oak trees were called Chestnut Oaks and were very hardy, growing mainly in harsh terrain such as existed along this trail. They were rough and almost stunted in appearance. We also often saw deer moving cautiously through the thick laurel as we moved along the trail. For some reason, deer seem less skittish of horses than they are of humans. One time I remember seeing a doe moving ahead of us with two fawns following her. It was a very memorable sight. I'm also pretty sure I saw my first pileated woodpecker along this trail. These woodpeckers are very large (perhaps 18 inches tall) and they are black and white with a red top on their head. When they peck on a tree the sound echoes throughout the forest.

After reaching Hall Road (I never knew the name in those days), we took a right and headed for Sutherland's Cliff and the Pond. We first went to the Cliff where I stood in awe of the beautiful panoramic view. We tied the horses and walked out on the rocks and just soaked it all in. Grayce had been there hundreds of times, of course, but this was my first view. The pond below with the swamp behind it, the other ponds and the fire tower in the distance and the unending trees in every direction formed a wilderness delight that still moves me to this day. On a clear day looking past the swamp, one could see the skyline of New York City sixty miles away. The Empire State building stands out in my mind as a most memorable sight.

We stayed there for a long time as Grayce told me about the many times she came to this place as a child. She described how she camped there overnight with the horses tied nearby and of picnics her family had while her brothers fished in the pond below. She kiddingly showed me a natural depression in the rock that she said had been worn out because she sat there so much over the years. Every time I visit that location, I think of that first time and my introduction to it.

After a while we went down to the pond and trotted the horses on the road that edged the pond. I always liked it when we ran the horses. We passed Sphagnum Pond, took a right at the four corners, and then passed the stone house, the fire tower, and Tamarack Pond before circling back passed Jim's Pond to the trail home. When we reached the field that the lady owned on Mine Hill Road, it was dusk. We saw deer grazing quietly as we passed through. By the time we reached the stable, it was dark, bringing to a close one of the most memorable days of my life.

SKYLINE OF NY CITY FROM SUTHERLAND'S CLIFF

# Discovery of the Spring near the Four Corners

One day as Grayce and I were riding along the Sutherland's Pond Road, she said that she wanted to show me a special place that we had not visited before. I was, of course, intrigued by the thought. When we reached the Four Corners, we took a left on the Continental Road. Shortly thereafter we followed a tiny trail on the left that was hardly visible. Not far in, we came to a spot where we saw some rocks with water flowing out from under them. Grayce explained that this was a natural spring that ran all year long even in the driest of times. I asked if it was safe to drink the water, to which she replied, of course. I got down immediately to taste it. Grayce showed me how to clear the leaves away and then wait for the water to settle before having a drink. Until that point in my life, I always thought of water as water but that changed that day. The water was so cold, pure, and refreshing that I made a point to stop at this little spring every time I was in the area, whether I was thirsty or not.

Years later after discovering William Thompson Howell's books about the Hudson Highland (Black Rock Forest is part of the Highlands) I found a reference to this little spring. Apparently he was introduced to the spring by a friend in a similar way that I was, and he had the same reaction. He first drank from it in August of 1909, some 45 years before I did. For some reason knowing that makes me feel a kinship to that author. Also, I'll add that he grew up on Montgomery Street in Newburgh which happens to be the same street that I lived on for a short time when I was a child.

Recently, I revisited the spring some sixty years later and found it to be neglected to the point that it was unrecognizable. It was totally filled with leaves, muck, and roots. With the help of my friend John Brady (former Black Rock Forest manager), I cleaned the spring so that it again flowed as before.

# Mountain Spring

When I was a boy in the days of yore,
I would roam through the mountains to explore,
Finding old paths, ancient rocks and far more.

Of all the places I discovered there,
The mountain spring was perhaps the most rare,
With its clear cool refreshing water fare.

Surrounded by rocks - a hole in the ground,
An endless supply of water did bound.
A purer delight could never be found.

I drank from it as often as I could
And every sweet time whenever I would,
All my taste buds would light up and feel good.

SPRING BEFORE CLEANING

SPRING AFTER CLEANING

# Upon My Return Sixty Years Later

After sixty years it sits there alone.
It speaks not a word not even a tone.
Undetectable except for the stone.

Covered with wet leaves - a hole of just muck,
Barely alive and way down on its luck.
A great blow to it has wrongly been struck.

What to do is the question I ponder.
How to renew its strength from down yonder.
So, I formed a plan – what could be sounder.

I hiked the mountain with shovel in hand,
To free the spring from roots, soil, and sand.
Digging and scraping, I removed every strand.

Not too long after the job was complete,
Water was flowing reversing defeat.
The years of neglect were put in retreat.

Finally, again it flows as before,
Bringing its pure water up from the floor
Renewing greatness – a treasure once more.

# Riding the Ridge Trail

The Ridge trail started at the Four Corners and proceeded along the ridge running parallel with Sutherland's Pond Road to Sutherland's Cliff. I never knew the real name of this trail or even if it had one but as kids, we always called it the Ridge Trail. I don't remember what Grayce called it, but I do remember that Grayce and I would follow it on horseback sometimes just for a change of scene. The trail itself was difficult to follow as it was not well marked. Blue Boy, who had been in the mountain many times over the years, knew exactly where the trail was even when we had difficulty following it. Grayce always said that I should never worry about getting lost in the mountains as long as I was riding Blue Boy, because he always knew the way home.

One day I put that theory to the test. On that day I was riding alone which was rare because Grayce was almost always with me in the mountains. Anyway, it was at the end of the day, and it was getting late. The Ridge Trail was the shortest way home but as I mentioned, it was not well marked, and it was rough in places. I decided to take it hoping that Blue Boy would bail me out if I got lost. Sure enough, part way along I lost the trail as it seemed to fade out of sight. I decided to let Blue Boy take over, still watching him to be sure that he didn't take me too far out of the way. I gave him his head, and he bolted forward with a quick determined pace. Before long I could see that we were on the right trail again. At that point I felt greatly relieved. Then, all of a sudden, he took a sharp turn down a steep old trail that I didn't know existed. With Grayce's words in my head, I let him continue to lead. It wasn't long before we turned onto a trail that I recognized as the way home. Blue Boy's short cut got us home in record time and before dark, and I was grateful.

.

OLD WEST POINT ROAD IN WINTER – PHOTO THANKS TO JOHN BRADY

# Riding the Old West Point Road

I knew of the Old West Point Road and something of its history, but I seldom traveled to that side of the Black Rock Forest because it was a long way from the stable. On this day, however, Grayce and I decided to go anyway. I think she just wanted me to see it, and it was well worth the trip. We rode the horses down Angola Road, crossed through the hay fields owned by Grover Cox and then up the Continental Road to 9W. Near the Storm King School we went through the tunnel under the highway. Before that day I didn't know there was a tunnel under 9W. As we passed under, the temperature dropped at least 10 degrees. I found that refreshing since the outside temperature on that summer day was quite high.

As we travelled up the winding road, Grayce gave me a history lesson of the roadway, explaining its importance in earlier days. At one point along a steep section, she showed me some logs that lay across the road. When she asked me what I thought they were, I told her that they looked like places to drain the water off the road. She told me that she thought that they were "Thank You Ma'am's". She could see, I assume, from the look on my face that I had never heard that term before, so she proceeded to explain. According to her, in the horse and carriage days when a horse was pulling the carriage up a steep incline, the driver would stop just passed one of these logs and let the carriage roll back to give the horse a rest. Grayce explained that the grateful horse would then turn back to the lady in the carriage and in his own way would say, Thank you Ma'am. To this day I'm not sure if there is any truth in what she said, but I still remember it.

When we reached the top of the mountain (White Horse Mountain), we stopped by the Upper Reservoir and had lunch. Afterwards we rode along the reservoir a short while following the old, abandoned section of the Old West Point Road. It was a little hard to follow as small trees and brush had started to fill in the unused road. I imagined what it must have been like when it was in full use before the Storm King Highway was built (1906). To this day I feel proud to have travelled on that most famous road before it disappeared into history. Today the section between the reservoir and West Point Military Academy has turned into woodland with just traces of the old road left.

We then backtracked, taking the White Oak Road passing the rifle range and Alex Meadow to the Continental Road. We stopped briefly at Arthur's Pond and Bog Meadow where Grayce told me a little about them, and then we headed home by Jim's Pond Road. As we passed Spy Rock and Eagles Cliff, she explained that we would ride to them on another day. As we passed Jim's Pond, I was struck by the black water snakes sunning themselves on the rocks. I think that every time I go to Jim's Pond I either see or at least think about those snakes.

PHOTO PREVIOUS PAGE: OLD WEST POINT ROAD ALONG THE UPPER RESERVOIR
BEFORE IT VANISHES INTO THE FOREST
PHOTO ABOVE: CONTINENTAL TRAIL NEAR THE WHITE OAK

We went right past Sutherland's Pond and the Cliff without stopping as it was getting late in the day. After following Hall Road for a while, we cut over on to Mine Hill Road and down the mountain to the stable on Angola Road. All in all, it was a long and memorable day.

# Riding the Continental Trail

The Continental Trail predated the Old West Point Road and in colonial times was the only passage through the forest from Washington's Headquarters in Newburgh to West Point. It passed right through the town of Cornwall along what is now known as the Continental Road. After crossing Route 9W, it enters the Black Rock Forest. At the entrance to the forest, it begins a rather steep long climb and then levels off as it passes the four corners on the way to West Point.

Grayce and I often followed this trail on our way to some particular destination. On this occasion, however, we made a point of following it from where it entered the forest to the gate at West Point. We saddled the horses and rode to the entrance of the forest by way of Grover Cox's fields. Then after crossing Route 9W, we continued along the Continental Trail through an area called Rock Areas and into the forest. I often think about the past travelers that followed this road. However, on this day we were purposely concentrating on following their footsteps. Certainly, General Washington came to mind but also other patriots like John Adams, Benjamin Franklin, Ethan Allen, and possibly Alexander Hamilton or Thomas Jefferson would have gone this way. It was after all, the main route to Fort Ticonderoga and New England. Even Benedict Arnold, as he was trading secrets with the British would have gone that way. I'm also sure that some of the famous outlaws like Claudius Smith that terrorized the Highlands also passed through. Claudius and his two sons rustled livestock and sold them to the British.

When we reached the spring at the top of the climb, we stopped for a cold, refreshing drink before moving on. Then we rode down past the stone house and the fire tower to the Big White Oak tree. I could just imagine what stories that tree could tell if it were able to talk. It was one of the few remaining old growth trees in the forest. It was probably there when Henry Hudson came up the river. No doubt General Washington's army marched by it many times. In more recent times (1900's), the author William Thompson Howell, Dr. Ernest Stillman (the former owner of the forest) and my grandfather Jacob Zoldak all passed it on their way through. I always feel like I am a part of history when I am near that tree.

We finally reached the West Point gate after stopping for a brief time at Bog Meadow Pond. Bog Meadow is a beautiful little woodland pond that is visible from the road. We then turned around and headed home while still discussing the history of this most famous landmark road. Our return was by way of Jim's Pond, Hall Road and down Secor's Hill to the stable.

THE STONE HOUSE (ONLY BUILDING IN THE FOREST) FORMERLY INHABITED BY ARTHUR BABCOCK

THE BIG WHITE OAK

# Trail Ride to Spy Rock and Eagles Cliff

On one of our Saturday trail rides, Grayce told me that she wanted to show me two of the highest points in the forest, Spy Rock and Eagles Cliff. I had heard her speak of these cliffs before, so I was excited by the prospect of visiting them. We had to leave earlier than usual because they were a good distance from the route we normally took though the forest. We entered the forest by way of Secor's Hill (Mine Hill Road), over the mountain trail to Hall's Road, to Sutherland's Pond Road, and then caught the Continental Road at the Four Corners. From there we rode all the way down past the White Oak to catch the trail up to the cliffs.

As we were on the Eagle Cliff trail, I kept wishing that I lived in a different time period. Grayce had told me many times of her childhood days when it was not uncommon to see nesting Bald Eagles in the rocks along the cliffs. William Thompson Howell's books referred to seeing eagles soaring down from the cliffs and what a spectacular sight it was to be looking down on them. In my day, however, eagles were rarely seen anywhere in the United States (the use of DDT almost brought them to extinction). Still, I remember hoping that on this day things would be different, and we would see one glide on by. That never happened, but we did see some Turkey Vultures circling around, which was pretty cool.

We first stopped at Spy Rock. After tying the horses, we walked out on the rocks and enjoyed the wonderful view as we looked down on Jim's Pond and then out to the south with the Hudson River in the distance. Grayce explained how signal fires were set ablaze from that location during the Revolutionary War. The fires served as warning to the Continental Army up the river that the British were coming.

VIEW OF JIM'S POND FROM THE TRAIL TO SPY ROCK.

The Pitch Pines on Spy Rock were inspiring as they seemed to blend in with the rocks, forming a most romantic scene. Pitch Pines grow very slowly and can endure extreme weather conditions. Some of the Pitch Pines in this location are over 150 years old. They grow out of the cracks and crevices of the rocks with their roots somehow gaining enough nourishment to survive. I wrote this poem trying to capture what appeared to me to be a love affair between these two unusual entities of nature.

# The Pitch Pine and the Cliff Rock

The Pitch Pine and the cliff rock
Form a most unlikely lover's pair,
Clinging each to the other,
A century of mutual care.

Through the summer's torturing heat
And the winter's harsh stormy blast,
They huddle themselves together
Tying a lover's knot that's fast.

OLD PITCH PINE GROWING OUT OF ROCK AT SPY ROCK

After enjoying the beauty of this place, we moved along to Eagles Cliff where the view was even more spectacular. Grayce told me that on a clear day one could see the Empire State Building similar to the view from Sutherland's Cliff. Unfortunately, on that day the clouds prevented us from seeing very far away. We saw no eagles and no Empire State Building but still a pretty great day. I have since gone back to see the city skyline, but still no eagles. After enjoying the scenery for a while, we mounted up again and rode down to Jim's Pond Road and back to Secor's Hill completing the loop ending a wonderful day.

VIEW FROM EAGLES CLIFF

In one of William Thompson Howell's books about hiking the Highlands, he mentions an experience at Eagles Cliff with a bobcat as he was camping there. I wrote this poem trying to catch the essence of the area.

LOOKING UP AT EAGLES CLIFF

# Eagles Cliff

Many old stories have been told,
About the cliffs there stout and bold
Majestic boulders hard and cold
Eagles Cliff

Soaring eagles seen gliding by
A look of grandeur in the sky
A lasting image to the eye.
Eagles Cliff

A scenic pond deep down below
Beautiful in the morning glow
And precious to all those who know
Eagles Cliff

Wild creatures roam through nearby
Squirrels, snakes, deer, and birds that fly,
Skunks, fox, and bobcats that cry.
Eagles Cliff

On a clear day over the green
A city skyline can be seen,
With sixty miles in between.
Eagles Cliff

Many travelers passing through
Enjoy the panoramic view
From these granite cliffs staunch and true.
Eagles Cliff

# A Final Word about Grayce Clark

I have many fond memories of my time working at the stable and the trail rides with Grayce. She not only taught me about Black Rock Forest but many life lessons as well. I learned how to be patient with the horses, and the other members of her small mini farm family (sheep, goats, and a donkey named Pedro). Also, she did small things for me such as gifting me my first baseball glove because she knew my family couldn't afford it. At Christmas one time she gave me a Christmas tree to take home because she knew it would help. Most mornings she would drive me part way to school on her way to work. She was a gym teacher in Newburgh. During the rides, we talked about the animals, of course, but also about other things like how I was doing in school or what sports I was going to get involved in. Then I moved into town, at age 15, and we kind of lost contact with one another. After high school I went off to college, got married, and had a family. I thought about the old days now and then but never tried to contact her.

One time later in life I decided to send her a letter. I knew that she had moved to Vermont to a farm that she purchased as a retirement home. I visited it once just before I moved into town, so I remembered the name of the town. Not knowing the exact address, I simply addressed it to that town, half expecting that it would be returned. To my surprise a few days later I got a phone call from her. We talked quite a long time trying to fill in 20 or 30 years of lost time. After that I drove to Vermont several times for a visit. During those visits we reminisced about the old days and how much we both had enjoyed them. Grayce died after 90 plus years of a meaningful life. I will always remember her fondly and with gratitude for all she taught me.

# SECTION TWO

## Teenage Years in Black Rock Forest after Moving into Town

After moving into town, I continued to visit Black Rock Forest as often as I could. I sometimes travelled on horseback from Pop Cowton's stable located near the entrance of the forest along Route 9W, but most often on foot. It was about a mile from my house to the nearest entrance, but I was young, so the distance didn't bother me much. The following thoughts/stories are from that time when I was 15 years old until I got married and left Cornwall.

# Camping at Sherwood's Cabin

Sometime during or just before the 1920's the Sherwood family (Matthew Sherwood) built a small mountain cabin, as they called it, part way up the mountain on the west side of Hall Road. The old photos show it in its prime with family members gathered there. However, when I visited it in the 1950's and 60's all that was left was the stone fireplace and a few of the original logs. The old photo with the Sherwood family in it is interesting because in the very front is Ann Roosevelt the youngest daughter of the former president of the United States. The two families were close in those days, and, in fact Sidney Sherwood, who is also in the photo, was said to be romantically involved with Ann. That relationship never materialized although it was apparently quite strong at one time.

SHERWOOD FAMILY AT THE CABIN WITH ANNE ROOSEVELT IN FRONT – FROM THE DAVID HARPER COLLECTION (CHS)

I found the cabin site quite interesting, and I visited it often as I traveled through the forest over the years. An old Cornwall resident, Russel Clark (Grayce's brother), who first showed me the location of the cabin, once told me a fascinating story about the cabin that I will never forget. He said that the cabin was at times used for hunting by the Sherwood men and probably others that they invited. In addition to hunting deer and other game that were located close to the cabin, at one point a mountain lion was shot near there. He said that it was the last mountain lion known to be in that region. That story made sense to me as I'm sure that mountain lions had to have visited the area at some point in its history. My grandfather always told me about the bobcats in the mountains but Russel Clark's tale was the only refer-ence to a mountain lion that I ever heard. Today, of course, there are still bobcats, deer, and other types of wildlife in that area including quite a few black bears. In my day, there were rumors of the existence of black bears, but I never saw one.

Now with all that as background, I would like to tell you about an experience that I had at the cabin around 1960 when I was a teenager. One day my friend Clyde (his real name was Vincent, but we called him Clyde) and I were anxious to get into the mountains after a long winter of absence due to excessive snow. It was April, and while there were still patches of snow on the ground, we thought we would spend part of the weekend there. We talked about it all week in school and planned to camp out on Friday night. On Friday it rained most of the day. The fore-cast called for clearing late in the day so we decided to go up after school anyway, thinking that the weather would only improve.

When school ended, we ran home, got our gear together and practically ran up the mountain. Our plan was to spend the night at Sherwood's cabin and then spend

Saturday roaming the woods. When we arrived at the cabin site, we tried to build a fire. With only a few matches and no dry kindling or firewood, we found it very difficult to start the fire. We almost got it going a couple of times, but eventually we ran out of matches and had to give up. By then it was getting really dark, and the temperature was dropping fast. We did have some food with us that did not require cooking, so we were not hungry.

Both Clyde and I were Boy Scouts, so we were not without knowledge on how to survive under difficult circumstances, but it was beginning to get very cold very fast. It wasn't long before we decided the best way to stay warm was to get into our sleeping bags. That worked well briefly, but it wasn't long before we felt cold again. As the temperature dropped through the night, we became more and more uncomfortable to the point that we wondered if we were going to survive. Keep in mind that sleeping bags in those days especially for kids of meager means were not that warm. We shivered through the night and only dozed off occasionally. We both agreed later that it was the longest night that we had ever experienced, and one that we never wanted to repeat.

The darkness was overwhelming with no moon or stars shining, and because we were far away from lights of any kind, it was pitch black. To add to our discomfort, the forest night sounds picked up as the night progressed. I had camped in the woods other times but not like this. Then suddenly around 3 or 4 am new sounds began. I was familiar with the screams that bobcats make from another experience in my life, but this was different because they were numerous and ever getting closer. Also, at this point, the story about the last cougar being shot close to where we were kept going through my head. I knew in my head that

A BLACK ROCK BOBCAT - PHOTO BY SCOTT LAPOINT (WILDLIFE BIOLOGIST FOR BRF)

bobcats seldom bother humans, but I wasn't sure that that was true of mountain lions. . I was sure they were bobcats, but what if I was wrong. All this time, Clyde was equally frightened, but we didn't talk much. The sounds seem to get closer and then move away only to come back again. They seemed almost on top of us at times. Screams on one side of us were answered by screams on the other side of us. We were two frightened kids trying to reassure each other that dawn was coming soon.

I can't tell you how glad we were to see the first sign of light. As the sun began to rise, the screams subsided. Eventually, the sun started to warm the forest. After a while we felt warm enough and safe enough to get out of our sleeping bags to start the day. We packed up our gear and got back on Hall Road and headed for Sutherland's Pond. I can't say that night was the worst in my life, but I'm pretty sure it made the top three. On the other hand, maybe it was number ONE.

# Clyde's Short Cut

Most of the time when we hiked to the Sutherland's Pond area, we either took the Continental Road to the four corners and then Sutherland's Pond Road or we branched off on Hall Road and came in from the back side. One day Clyde, who was a couple of years older than me, said he thought that if we climbed over the ridge between Hall Road and Sutherland's Pond Road that we could save time. That sounded feasible to me. On the next trip, we tried it. The climb up to the ridge was difficult but we made it to Sutherland's Pond in what seemed like a faster time. From then on, we took "Clyde's Short Cut" every time we went to Sutherland's Pond. One day as we were making the hard climb to the ridge, I said to Clyde that I was beginning to wonder if this was the fastest way after all. He was sure it was but agreed to try an experiment the next time we went to Sutherland's Pond. When that day came Clyde took his short cut and I went the traditional way to the four corners and Sutherland's Pond Road. We agreed to meet at the campsite at the end of the pond. When I arrived at the campsite, I expected to see Clyde waiting because on the trip I had come to the conclusion that he was probably right. Imagine my surprise when Clyde had not yet arrived. About 10 minutes later Clyde wandered in. We had a good laugh and never took Clyde's short cut again. I will say this though, I never go to Sutherland's Pond without thinking of "Clyde's Short Cut".

# The View from Black Rock

Black Rock (after which I assume the forest was named) is accessible by following a path that starts near the Four Corners. The view from this location is amazing as one can see all the way up the Hudson River on a clear day. In the days before the Newburgh-Beacon Bridge was built, the ferries were visible as they crossed the river. As a kid I didn't visit Black Rock as much as I did as an adult, probably because it was a little out of the way from our fishing and camping excursions.

At the top of Black Rock, the combination of the rocks and the pine trees form a delightful sight. The pines seem to sprawl out hugging the rocks as if they are meant to be together. Part of the reason for this beautiful entanglement, I'm sure, is because of the harsh winds that at times blow over the rocks at that elevation, stunting the growth of the pines. William Thompson Howell refers to these pines in his books written in the early 1900's, so this beautiful relationship has been going on for a long time.

PHOTO ABOVE: VIEW FROM BLACK ROCK

I've learned since that these amazing pines are called Pitch Pines and that they are over 150 years old. Some of them are growing in the cracks in the rocks. You would think that they could never survive under these conditions, but they do. This arrangement of Pitch Pines and rock is also found on Eagles Cliff and Spy Rock, as I mentioned earlier.

PITCH PINES AMONG THE CLIFF ROCKS

# Slipping and Sledding on
# The Sawmill Road (Hulse Road)

The Sawmill Road, called Hulse Road on the map (probably named after the family that once owned the land) runs from Route 9W up to the Four Corners. We called it the Sawmill Road because there was an old sawmill at the base of the road just before the steep incline into the forest. It is one of the major access roads and by far the most difficult to use because it is so steep. Most of the time we used the Continental Trail to go in from the Route 9W side to avoid the steep incline of the Sawmill Road. However, we often came home that way because it was faster. The reason it was faster was that we could run downhill at full speed and not really get very tired.

There were, however, a few turns on the way that had to be carefully maneuvered or one would go flying off into the woods. In the winter, it was even more tricky and more fun because most of the road was covered with ice. We found that we

THE TURN ON THE SAWMILL ROAD

could run and slide all the way down and enjoy ourselves at the same time. The most difficult turn in the road to maneuver was located about halfway down. Fortunately, a tree branch protruded out into the road at this location. We would simply grab that branch at full speed and use it to swing around the turn. On occasion one of us would miss the branch and wind up tumbling into the woods. The rest of us would have a good laugh at the poor guy's expense. Strangely enough, no one ever got seriously hurt.

Sometimes we would bring our sleighs (Flexible Flyers) and climb all the way to the top just to come down at breakneck speeds and then do it all over again. The turns in the road, as well as the ice, caused many accidents and departures into the woods. Each followed by a roar of laughter. I remember one time Clyde going off into the woods and hitting a tree. Just as he was getting up and shaking the snow off himself, I went off the road and blasted right into him. We both had a great laugh and then got back on the road to continue on our way.

# Sutherland's Cliff (Echo Rock)

Sutherland's Cliff is probably my favorite spot in the forest. Just looking down onto the pond with all its natural beauty would be enough, but there is so much more to it. On a clear day, you can see most of the forest, including some of the ponds and the fire tower in the distance. From that vantage point there is no sign

VIEW FROM SUTHERLAND'S CLIFF

of civilization in any direction, only forest. I spent many wonderful hours lying on the rocks enjoying the sunshine and the view.

There are three trails to get to the cliff. The least used comes across the ridge parallel with Sutherland's Pond Road. This trail in my time was hard to follow because it was overgrown and not clearly marked. We always referred to it as the Ridge Trail as I mentioned earlier. A second trail cuts off from Hall Road and catches the Ridge Trail midway through. This one is the fastest way to get to the cliff, coming from Mine Hill Road. My favorite trail, however, is the one that leads up from the end of the pond. It leads through dense mountain laurel, which is always beautiful, but especially so during the spring when it is in bloom. I almost always encounter deer along that trail as well as a grouse flush or two. I would even walk the longer distance when coming over from Mine Hill Road just to take that trail to the cliff. I would visit Sutherland's Cliff every time that I was in the area, and I never got bored with the hike or the view.

There is a reason that Sutherland's Cliff is called Echo Rock and this story will tell you why. Laura (my wife) and I hiked into the forest from Mine Hill Road one day during our younger years, following the steep trail over the mountain. We parked the car in a pull off just after making that hair pin turn. As we were getting out of the car, two huge black dogs (Newfoundlands, I think) greeted us. We assumed they lived in one of the houses nearby. They were quite friendly and full of energy. As we started up the trail, we figured that they would return home after a while. However, to our surprise they stayed with us the whole way into the forest. The steep trail is challenging but worth the trip because the view of the valley is breathtaking along the way. Once we reached Hall Road, we followed it until we came to the trail that led to the Cliff. All the time the dogs followed us seeming to know exactly where we were going. We reached the Cliff about lunch time, so we sat in Grayce's spot and ate the sandwiches we had packed.

Suddenly, the dogs started barking with a low-pitched booming bark that only these dogs can make. The echo coming back was equally loud, filling the air with sounds that I'm sure could be heard for miles. The dogs knew exactly what they were doing and totally enjoyed it. After a while they got tired of barking and settled down. As we left the cliff to head down to the pond, they took off the other way and headed home. We never saw them again. They had apparently stayed with us just to enjoy hearing themselves on Echo Rock. I admit I enjoyed it too.

I would occasionally camp out in the cliff area, and when I did, I often thought of Grayce telling me about how she and her friends would spend the night there with the horses. She said that she would unsaddle them and let them graze overnight on the scattered grass that grew there. I would have liked to have done that.

I almost always visited the cliff in the warm weather. I guess because I was always ice fishing on the pond in the winter and the cliffs didn't have the same appeal. However, I remember one winter day being there when a snow squall came up suddenly. The snow was pelting down so hard it was hard for me to see. The view looking over the cliff was a harsh reminder that nature occasionally had a fierce side and had to be respected.

SUTHERLAND'S POND VIEWED FROM THE CLIFF ABOVE

# Sutherland's Pond and the Power of a Good Name

There are so many stories that I could tell you about Sutherland's Pond. The first time that I can remember visiting the pond was with Grayce Clark as I mentioned earlier. I was very anxious to go that day knowing that I would finally see the place that my grandfather had talked about during my visits with him. My grandfather had cancer and died a few years later but we talked about the pond often before he died.  When I first saw the pond, I was in awe of its natural beauty. It was just as he had described it. As we visited the cliff and later rode along the shore, I felt closer than ever to him. Other people I knew that had travelled that way as well had told me wonderful stories about family picnics and the fishing trips when huge fish were caught there.

I love the story in William Thompson Howells book about the Sutherland's family funeral on the day that Fort Montgomery was attacked during the Revolutionary War. All the neighbors who had come to show their respect to the deceased suddenly left in the middle of the funeral when they heard gunfire in the distance. They hurried home to protect their property as the story was told.

After that first time visiting the pond, I returned many times during my teenage years, first on horseback and then hiking and camping with my friends. From then on until I went away to college, I spent many weekends and summer days in the forest, most often at Sutherland's Pond. During my adult years, I returned almost any time I'd visit Cornwall. I feel like it is part of who I am.

There was always something to do at the pond. In the summer we mostly fished and camped out. At night we built a campfire where we told stories and just enjoyed being together. In the winter we would go ice fishing or exploring the backside of the pond. The beaver hut near the swamp side of the pond always had activity around it. Beavers were very scarce in those days so being able to visit a place where they actually existed was a real treat. Later, when I returned as an adult, a colony of otters had also moved in. Their fun-filled antics are always fun to watch.

One day when I was in my teenage years, Clyde and I discovered a boat hidden in the brush alongside the pond. We used it to fish the other side of the pond

OLD CAMPSITE ON SUTHERLAND'S POND

where we could not get to easily. We had no oars, so we cut some long poles to help us maneuver the boat through the water. It all worked out pretty well, and we caught more fish than usual.

One day a man caught us using the boat. We figured we were in big trouble. He told us that the boat belonged to him and some other men from the Black Rock Fish and Game Club. He said that they had hauled the boat up there for their own use and didn't expect anyone else to use it. He seemed quite angry. He then turned to us and asked our names. When I told him my name, he seemed to recognize it. He then asked me if I was related to Old Jake. When I told him that Jake was my grandfather, his whole attitude changed. After a little more discussion, he said that I was welcome to use the boat any time that he and his friends weren't using it. It's amazing the power a good name has. We spent the rest of the summer using the boat every time we went fishing.

THE ORIGINAL SIGN FROM 65 YEARS AGO AT THE EDGE OF SPHAGNUM POND

LAUREL CAVE

# Fishing and Camping at Sphagnum Pond and the Cave

After leaving Sutherland's Pond heading back toward the four corners, there is another pond called Sphagnum Pond. At the end of the pond is a dam with a spill-way flowing over it. We always found this pond harder to fish than Sutherland's Pond except in the winter. Also, it had a sign near the entrance to the dam that said "reservoir: no trespassing or swimming" so we wondered if we would get in trouble for fishing there. The sign didn't mention fishing, but we still wondered. For some reason it didn't bother us as much in the winter, probably because there were fewer people in the forest then.

There are a couple of stories that I would like to share about this pond. Down near the far end of the pond away from the dam was what we referred to as the

43

THE CLIFF ABOVE THE CAVE

cave. It was more like a place in the rocks that was sheltered by a huge leaning rock that covered a hollowed-out area. At one end, there was a fairly large opening and on the other a very small outlet. It was a good place to camp because there was room enough for 2 or 3 kids to sleep out of the weather. A fire could be built near the back end with the smoke going out of the small outlet. To get to the cave required travelling through dense mountain laurel which made it even more isolated and unapproachable.

Back from the cave and the water's edge was a cliff. That cliff was a good place to have a snowball fight in the winter. On one occasion I went up on the ledge along the cliff and started throwing snowballs into the mouth of the cave. I really had the guys in the cave pinned down. Their snowballs fell short of hitting me because of the height of the cliff. That advantage didn't last long, however, because they came out of the cave with rocks which, unlike snowballs, had enough velocity to reach my location. The snowball fight ended shortly thereafter with me leaving my location in fear of losing my balance on the ledge.

One night when Clyde and I and another friend, who shall remain nameless, were camping in the cave, the friend got up to go down by the pond.  He walked to the water's edge and stood on a rock gazing across the pond. After he left, we decided to scare him a little in a way that only immature teenage boys would think of. We happened to have with us on this trip a 20-gauge shot gun that I had purchased earlier that year. We blasted the gun off in the air, shattering the silence of the night with what seemed like unusual loudness. Well, the poor guy fell off the rock and into the pond as soon as the gun went off. Young boys can be cruel. The two of us had a good laugh. Our friend saw the humor in it eventually.

ROCK ALONG THE POND OUTSIDE THE CAVE

Not far from the cave was an island that was quite close to the shore. It had almost a moat-like waterway channel surrounding it on one side and could only be accessed from the shore by walking carefully across a couple of logs that stretched the distance (about 8 feet) between the shore and the island. We found that island a fun place to go out to and play.

In the winter we always used it as a hiding place for our spud because of its remote location. A spud is the common name for an ice chisel used for cutting holes in the ice during ice fishing. An old hollow log on the island was just long enough to hide the spud. The reason that we liked having the spud there was that we didn't have to carry it up the mountain every time we went fishing. It was made of steel, so it was quite heavy. I think it is possible that the spud is still on that Island although I'm sure the log is long gone.

THE MOAT LIKE CHANNEL AROUND THE ISLAND

On one of our ice fishing trips, we were fishing down near the cave end of the pond and having a very poor day of it. We were there several hours and had only caught a small yellow perch or two that we threw back. The perch seemed to run in schools so if we caught one we were likely catch another the next time we put the tip-up back in the water. To avoid wasting our bait, we would simply keep the tip-up out of the water for a while until the school of perch moved on. Just before we were going to leave the pond at the end of the day, I got a flag on one of the tip-ups. It's always exciting to get a flag, but especially on a slow fishing day. I ran over to the hole and started pulling in the line. I knew immediately by the feel of the line that it was another perch and sure enough it was. Going along with our usual pattern I threw the tip-up on the ice debating whether to just pack it up for the day. I decided to wait a couple of minutes and then try it one more time since we didn't need to worry about running out of bait that late in the day. After a few minutes I dropped the line back in the water and set the tip-up. As I was turning to go away, I heard the flag spring up in the air. I thought to myself those damn perch. Disgusted, I went over and yanked on the line to set the hook but this time the fish pulled back. I then knew it was no perch. I yelled to Clyde that I had a good one as I continued to haul it in. As it got closer to the surface, I could see that it was big. It turned out to be the biggest pickerel that we ever caught in that pond. Needless to say, we walked home happy that night.

# Catfish in the Sphagnum Swamp

Just below the dam at Sphagnum Pond is a large swamp. For the most part we would avoid the swamp because it was hard to get into without getting very wet and dirty. There were snapping turtles in the swamp, but they were only of mild interest to us unless we came upon a particularly large one. Then we would venture over to have a look.

In the winter the swamp was quite accessible because of the freezing conditions. On one winter trip Clyde and I came to a small shallow pool in the middle of the swamp that was covered with very clear ice. The water underneath was running so the ice was not very thick. It was, however, thick enough to hold our weight while crossing it. As we moved along, we could see through the ice that there were catfish just under the surface. It looked like there were thousands of them of all sizes. They ranged from a couple of inches to a foot in length. With an axe we cut a hole through the ice and the fish bubbled up to the surface. Then, using a camp shovel that we had with us, we shoveled about 200 of them onto the ice. I knew that my family loved to eat catfish, especially ones that are about 7 to 9 inches long (longer than that the taste diminishes) so I decided to take some home. Clyde wasn't interested in taking any but was willing to help me. I always had with me a stringer to carry home any fish we caught, so we picked out exactly 50 fish of the desired length and put them on the stringer. The others we pushed back into the water.

The trip home was laborious as carrying that many fish was not easy. Things didn't get any better when I got home either. They had to be cleaned, skinned, and packed in the freezer. It was worth it though because we had catfish to eat all winter. Interestingly enough we returned to the same spot two weeks later and all the catfish were gone. We never saw anything like that again.

PHOTO FOLLOWING PAGE:  SPHAGNUM SWAMP – PHOTO THANKS TO JOHN BRADY

# Climbing the Fire Tower

This metal framed structure was located near the stone house formerly inhabited by Arthur Babcock and close to Tamarack Pond. I'm not sure when the fire tower was erected (perhaps in the 1930's) but it was in a deteriorated state when I was roaming the forest. The metal framing was solid, but the wooden steps and platforms were rotted through. I remember on several occasions climbing to the top having to be careful of rotted wood. As time passed, the lower section of the stairway was removed to prevent anyone from climbing the tower. As you might expect, that didn't deter teenage boys like us. We simply climbed the outside of the tower until we were able to get to the stairs. It was a challenge but well worth the effort. The view was most impressive because we could see for miles in all directions. One thing that impressed me was that nowhere was there any sign of civilization, only trees, ponds, and natural beauty.

THE FIRE TOWER

I would guess that the fire that my grandfather fought in the 1930's was spotted from that tower (there was an earlier one made of wood so I'm not totally sure). Today the fire tower has been repaired and looks like it probably did after it was first built. I had the pleasure of climbing it recently with my son and with the help of the retired forest manager, John Brady, who allowed us access. It brought back so many memories that I was inspired to write this poem.

# The Fire Tower

FIRE TOWER VIEWED FROM
TAMARACK POND

Up on a knoll above a forest pond,
Overlooking trees below and beyond,
Is a fire tower that way back when
Was built to observe the woodlands within.

Made from sturdy iron, steel, and some wood,
Bettering the test of time, there it stood.
Day and night, a sentinel it would stand,
Protecting all the sacred forest land.

Generations of watchers used its view,
To discover flames or some smoke anew.
Then rallying a crew of men to send,
They brought the forest blaze to an end.

Now it stands there as an old, outdated shrine
From days that are just fashioned in one's mind.
But still, some remember that from way back when
Its job to the forest was to attend.

Though it's been refitted for these current days
With electronics made for modern ways,
The beauty of its awesome form and grace
Goes back to its original time and place.

# The Snakes at Jim's Pond

Jim's Pond is a small man-made pond along Jim's Pond Road which connects Sutherland's Pond and the Continental Road. The pond is named after Jim Babcock who was the manager of the forest for many years back in the 1910's, 20's and 30's. I'm sure my grandfather and he were friends because they were from the same era. I didn't go to this pond very often for two reasons. First it was a long hike to get to unless I was on horseback. Grayce and I rode by fairly often during my early years. The other reason was that the shoreline rocks seemed to always have large black water snakes sunning themselves on them. Somehow spending much time there didn't appeal to me. The pond has an attractive setting, however, with the cliffs above it. I much preferred to view it from those cliffs above.

JIM'S POND

THE SHORE ALONG TAMARACK POND WHERE WE FOUND THE BOAT

# Catching the Big One at Tamarack Pond

Most of the time our fishing excursions were to either Sutherland's Pond or Sphagnum Pond, probably because they were closer to home. However, one day Clyde and I walked over to Tamarack just to try it. We first fished down by the point off a big rock, where we caught a couple of pickerel. That was enough to perk our interest for future fishing trips although Tamarack was hard to fish from shore because of all the bushes (mostly blueberries) around the edge. From the rock we observed the island and a large osprey nest built in an old tree on it. Ospreys are large fish-eating birds similar to eagles and every bit as impressive. The nest was inactive at the time but still cool to see. From there we decided to head towards the fire tower located on the other side of the pond. As we approached the pond

53

VIEW OF TAMARACK POND FROM THE FIRE TOWER

from the other side, we saw a rowboat on the shore. That surprised us since boats of any kind were very rare on the ponds in those days. It was late in the day, so we decided to check it out further on another day.

The next time we climbed the mountain to go fishing we went directly to the spot where we had seen the boat. Sure, enough it was still there so we cut a couple of saplings to use as poles and loaded our fishing equipment in the boat. Keep in mind that we were kids so our fishing tackle only consisted of a rod and reel, two or three dare devil spoons, and maybe a bobber, some sinkers and a few hooks. After looking around to be sure no one saw us, we pushed off into the pond. We tried several spots before heading out toward the island. The area around the island was peculiar in that it was surrounded by old tree stumps just below the surface. In those days the ponds in Black Rock were mostly fished out. So to catch a large fish was unusual. We caught a couple of pickerel about 12 or 14 inches long which was a pretty good catch for us. Then suddenly Clyde who was in the front of the boat asked me to look for his line near the back where I was. He thought he had hooked one of the roots on a stump. As I looked down, I yelled to him that he wasn't caught on a stump at all but rather had the biggest pickerel on that I had ever seen. It took the two of us to haul it in the boat. When we finally did, it kept flipping around so much that we had to stuff it under the seat to keep it from jumping out. We were so excited that we poled back to shore immediately and carried our prize catch home. Needless to say, we kept coming back to Tamarack until someone took the boat away. We caught a couple of other big fish but none like the one on that first day.

# Visiting Mineral Springs

I find it hard to think of Mineral Springs as part of the Black Rock Forest although I guess it officially is. It is accessible from Mineral Springs Road off Angola Road. My family had enjoyed this beautiful location long before I was born. My grandparents often took their family (my father and his brothers) there for picnics. I'm pretty sure my grandfather caught brook trout in the pools along the brook.

I'm always impressed with the temperature drop as you approach the Falls. The temperature is at least 10 degrees lower than it is outside of that location on a warm summer day. The large falls just above the pool at the base is certainly impressive, but I also enjoy climbing to a place just above that falls to a smaller falls that is also beautiful. Sometimes if I am by myself, I will follow the brook through the forest and up the mountain to where it drains out of Sutherland's Pond.

When I was dating, I would take my girlfriends there when I wanted to impress them, and it always worked. The last one is now my wife of 58 years, and we still stop in when we are in town. Also, over the years whenever we were visiting with friends, that is one stop that we always made knowing our friends will enjoy its beauty. It's amazing how accessible this place is and yet many local people are unfamiliar with it. For me it's a place to connect with my ancestors through memories.

# Mineral Springs

Over the rocks she flows with grace,
Ever moving with rapid haste
Toward the deep pool down at the base.
Tumbling - tumbling - tumbling.

Flowing from a pond way up high
On through the forest on the fly
Over and over rolling by.
Tumbling - tumbling - tumbling

While standing there along her shore
One can feel all her power soar,
And listen to her rushing roar.
Tumbling – tumbling - tumbling

Then through the ages she ignites,
The inner soul that she excites,
Whenever she comes into sight
Tumbling - tumbling - tumbling

PHOTO LEFT PAGE:  THE LOWER FALLS AT MINERAL SPRINGS –
PHOTO THANKS TO BOB MCCUE
PHOTO ABOVE: THE UPPER FALLS AT MINERAL SPRINGS

# SECTION THREE

## Visiting the Forest with John Brady
## in Preparation for this Book

JOHN BRADY (BRF MANAGER FOR 40 YEARS)

I hadn't planned to add another section to this book, but while visiting the forest with my son and my wife (on different days), and with the help of John Brady (the forest manager from 1979 until recently) to take photographs, I decided that I had more to say. Even though my years predated John's time in the forest, we found we had a lot in common and could learn from one another. The forest had changed so much over time that I was thankful for John's assistance in getting around, not to mention that he had keys to the gates and a truck to drive us close to our destinations. Some of the time he stayed with us and other times he dropped us for a few hours and picked us up later at a predetermined location. We got together 3 times with John in 2022. The first two times we visited some predetermined locations to take photographs or a location that John thought we might be interested in. The third time John and I went alone into the forest to clean some springs that had been neglected over the years. On all three of these trips, I enjoyed not only his company but his enthusiasm and love of Black Rock Forest.

# Visiting the Site Where the Black Rock Hermit Lived

I was surprised to learn from John that a hermit by the name of Victor Martineck had lived in the forest during my years roaming there. He apparently had a small shack not far from Sutherland's Pond. When we visited the site, we found the remains of the cabin and pots, pans, buckets, and other signs of his lodging place. There was also a small hand dug pool that he used as a water supply. The entire site had been abandoned for many years. It's funny that in all the time I was in the woods, I never saw him. I'm willing to bet that he saw me, however.

"From what John told me, he had permission from Dr. Stillman to live there during the warmer months of the year. In the winter he returned to his home in civilization. I guess you could say that he was a part time hermit. The story of his life is rather a sad tale, particularly near the end of his 60 years in the forest. By the end he was quite paranoid and so much so that he destroyed his own cabin to keep it from falling into the hands of someone that he perceived as his enemy. The following excerpt is from a short autobiography written by Victor Martineck giving an idea of his personality and where and why he sought refuge in the forest.

THE SITE WHERE THE HERMIT LIVED

*"In June 97 I was born. A product of my parents, I did not evolve from their genes. We were strangers. According to their lights they were good parents. 75 years ago the concept of child-psychology did not exist; the offspring was not an individual. He just grew up as does a young carrot; its root meets a pebble, deviates, the trunk becomes an "aberrant". At 10, inflammation of meninges and backbone marrow greatly affected me for years. This and preceding trends made me frail, diffident, and ill adjusted. Tallest and weakest, I was but of contempt, ridicule by my robust schoolfellows. (Now almost all dead.)*

*I became an introvert, an autist, a Kaspar Milquestoast. These labels marked my whole life. Society deals with psychology, not with decalogue. It searches out the mild Achilles' soft spot, pierces it. My whole life reaped abuse.*

*My own self and the woods offered escape. I found comfort in the nonhumanous nature where animals openly kill and trick for the sake of survival but are never humanous, beastly. These I admire.*

*During one of my lone cross-country/ compass hikes from Bear Mountain to Schunemunk Mt. I came at nightfall upon the Odell cabin. It was swaying; all its elements were neither plumb or level. Rain-bound I spent 3 nights, and 2 days. Weeks later I found it collapsed.*

*From its lumber, down the slope, my cabin arose. That was in 1927, I was younger. About the landownership I did not think. When informed, I begged Dr. Stillman to kindly make an exception to the rule of forbidding permanent camps. His generous reply is enclosed.*

*There I found happiness. The trees, the animals did not hurt, sneer at me. I loved the camp."*

This sad account goes on and on, but I will stop here and simply say that this man represents to me why some individuals go into isolation. I wonder if my grandfather knew him.

# The Continental Spring

The Continental Spring was another site that John shared with me that I had never been to before. We visited it on the day that we were in the forest cleaning springs. We had just finished cleaning the Four Corners Spring and were moving on to the second of the four springs we worked on that day. The area where the spring was located was off Sawmill Road (Hulse Road) not far from the Four Corners and along an abandoned section of the old Continental Road. We entered the woods and followed the old road. Walking was very difficult because many trees had fallen across it over the years. When we finally arrived at the site, we only found a place where the area was wet but no clear spring location. It was at the base of a rock formation.

Using the tools that we brought with us, we cleared the area, trying to locate the actual spring opening. We narrowed it down to a few square feet where the ground was particularly wet. We were able to clear a space where a purposely laid rock path led to the spring. We surmised that this stone path had been used in colonial times to keep the people that came there from getting their feet wet. We also looked around for any old artifacts that may have been left there over the years. The only things we found were a couple of pieces of pottery (which turned out to be only about 50 years old) and a very smooth, round brownish colored stone that seemed out of place in that location.

After about an hour of hard work, we decided to move on to the other two springs that we wanted to work on that day with the thought that we would return another time. I did feel that while we were there we were on ground once used by people from colonial times, perhaps even General Washington himself with his horse being watered there. I do hope to return.

We cleaned the Babcock Spring and worked on one other before calling it a day. I find myself fascinated with all of the springs in the forest knowing that they were once used by the old families before the forest was formed.

PHOTO RIGHT: CONTINENTAL SPRING SITE

GRANDPA AT THE CAVE

# Rediscovering the Cave (Laurel Cave) on Sphagnum Pond

The cave was one place in the forest that John had never been. Since I had not been there either for many years, I thought it might be hard to locate. I was partly right. When we were young, we always approached it from Sutherland's Pond Road by crossing the dam and fighting our way through the thick laurel. John suggested that we take a different approach this time because he said the dam was too dangerous to cross in its deteriorated state. So, we went in from Chatfield Road, which turned out to be difficult but shorter in distance.

Finding the cave was less difficult than I thought it might be, other than the difficulty of getting through the thick laurel and having to climb over the high, rough boulders. From the other direction, the laurel would have been as thick but less boulders. Anyway, I was surprised to discover that my memory brought me relatively close to the location. After a little wandering around the area, I recognized the small opening to the cave partly covered with brush. To get to the main entrance, we had to climb over the boulders and down to the other side. With some effort and help from my son, I got to the other side.

Entering the cave brought back many wonderful memories from my teenage years. It looked exactly the same except for the many leaves that had blown in over time. The rocks located around it were just as I remembered them. The trees were either much larger or gone but over all very much the same. John thought it should have a name and suggested Bill's Cave, but I felt that since I was only one of several boys that frequented it back in the 1950's and 60's and perhaps other boys over the years knew of it, that name was inappropriate. As I thought about it, the name Laurel Cave seemed like a good name to me.

# The Laurel Cave

Deep within the Black Rock Forest
Away from the local tourist
Is a special place that I know
Beneath some rocks way down below.

Hidden within this forest green,
Its location cannot be seen.
Deeply entwined and out of sight,
Covered with twisted laurel tight.

Found by boys many years ago,
For whom it had a certain glow.
A respite where they all could stay,
Not being bothered while they play.

They built a fire at one end,
Giving them warmth and light within
There these boys camped out all night,
With burdens few, their hearts were light.

Then exploring the cliffs up high
New adventures were found to try.
Climbing out on a ledge with care,
Jumping to a tree on a dare.

These boys fished the pond down below,
Summer, Spring, Fall and in the snow,
Catching fish but oh - so much more
Forming memories by the score.

That old cave is still there today,
But the boys have all gone away.
Although some return now and then
It's not the same as it had been.

The pond is there – the cliff is too.
The laurels still hard to get through.
Now the old cave is full of leaves,
Empty beneath the brush and trees

Perhaps someday - I know not when,
This Laurel Cave will live again.
When boys (or girls) will enter there
And of its treasure they will share.

ALEX MEADOW

ARTHUR'S POND – PHOTO THANKS TO JOHN BRADY

# Some Final Thoughts

In conclusion, I would like to say a few more words about the forest and our time spent there in 2022. Over the years the forest had changed dramatically, but the places that I remembered and loved were still there. The White Oak was still there even though the area around it was almost unrecognizable to me. The Stone House looked about the same, but the surroundings had changed some. The Fire Tower actually looked much better with its repairs. The Sherwood's Cabin site hadn't changed much at all. The Pine Grove near Tamarack Pond had aged greatly, the swamp below Sphagnum Pond was very different. Some of the old roads were grown in, but there were many more hiking trails than I remembered. The riding trail entrance off Mine Hill Road was gone, but the outlet onto Hall Road was still there. The ponds looked much the same. The views from Sutherland's Cliff, Spy Rock, Eagles Cliff and Black Rock were still spectacular. The Pitch Pines in these locations were recognizable and comforting to me.

I was very glad that I had some time to spend with my son Will in the forest. This was the first time since his teenage years that he had been there. Our plan is to return with his son (my grandson), in the near future. When that happens, Jacob, "Young Jake", will be the fifth generation of our family to experience the grandeur of this most wonderful forest. I'm sure that old Jake, my father (Joseph), and, perhaps, Grayce will be with us in spirit.


Love as always,
Grandpa

# ACKNOWLEDGEMENTS

John Brady (former manager of the Black Rock Forest) for contributing photos
and acting as a guide in the forest.

Scott Lapoint (Wildlife Biologist) for contributing a photograph.

David Harper Collection of the Cornwall Historical Society
for contributing a photograph.

Bob McCue for contributing a photograph.

Betsy Clark for contributing a photograph.

Will Zoldak for contributing photographs.